# ✦ WORDS THAT CHANGED AMERICA ✦

# JOHN F. KENNEDY

## THE INAUGURAL ADDRESS

### INTRODUCTION BY
### CAROLINE KENNEDY

---

### THIS WAS AMERICA, 1960
### ELIZABETH PARTRIDGE

---

### ADDRESS ON CIVIL RIGHTS

---

### ADDRESS AT AMERICAN UNIVERSITY

VIKING
An Imprint of Penguin Group (USA) Inc.

VIKING
Published by Penguin Group
Penguin Group (USA) Inc., 345 Hudson Street,
New York, New York 10014, U.S.A.
Penguin Group (Canada), 90 Eglinton Avenue East, Suite 700, Toronto,
Ontario, Canada M4P 2Y3 (a division of Pearson Penguin Canada Inc.)
Penguin Books Ltd, 80 Strand, London WC2R 0RL, England
Penguin Ireland, 25 St Stephen's Green, Dublin 2, Ireland
(a division of Penguin Books Ltd)
Penguin Group (Australia), 250 Camberwell Road, Camberwell,
Victoria 3124, Australia (a division of Pearson Australia Group Pty Ltd)
Penguin Books India Pvt Ltd, 11 Community Centre, Panchsheel Park,
New Delhi – 110 017, India
Penguin Group (NZ), 67 Apollo Drive, Rosedale, North Shore 0632,
New Zealand (a division of Pearson New Zealand Ltd.)
Penguin Books (South Africa) (Pty) Ltd, 24 Sturdee Avenue,
Rosebank, Johannesburg 2196, South Africa

Penguin Books Ltd, Registered Offices: 80 Strand,
London WC2R 0RL, England

First published in 2010 by Viking,
a member of Penguin Group (USA) Inc.

1   3   5   7   9   10   8   6   4   2

PHOTO CREDITS:
Front cover: Diamond Images/Getty Images
p. iv: Cecil Stoughton, in the John F. Kennedy Presidential Library and Museum, Boston
p. 12: John F. Kennedy Presidential Library and Museum, Boston

Printed in the USA    Set in Minister Book    Book design by Jim Hoover

**For more information, please visit www.jfklibrary.org**

# CONTENTS

Introduction
**CAROLINE KENNEDY** . . . . . . . . . . . . . . 1

The Gift Outright
**ROBERT FROST** . . . . . . . . . . . . . . . . . . . 11

The Inaugural Address
**JOHN F. KENNEDY** . . . . . . . . . . . . . . . . . 13

This Was America, 1960
**ELIZABETH PARTRIDGE** . . . . . . . . . . . . 22

Report to the American People
on Civil Rights (excerpts)
**JOHN F. KENNEDY** . . . . . . . . . . . . . . . . . 38

Commencement Address
at American University (excerpts)
**JOHN F. KENNEDY** . . . . . . . . . . . . . . . . . 50

# INTRODUCTION
## CAROLINE KENNEDY

**ON JANUARY 20, 1961,** when my father, John F. Kennedy, took the oath of office as the thirty-fifth president of the United States, the world began to change. The youngest man ever elected president, he was also the first Catholic, and the first born in the twentieth century. A Democratic senator and congressman, he was a handsome naval war hero, a Pulitzer Prize–winning author, one of nine children of a wealthy and well-educated family, with a beautiful and intelligent wife and two young children.

My father, known as Jack, was the second oldest of four boys and five girls. As a child, he was skinny and almost always sick. His brothers and sisters used to joke that any mosquito that bit him was taking a huge risk—with some of Jack's blood the mosquito was almost sure to die! As a result of spending so much time recuperating, my father became a voracious reader. He was very smart, but he didn't care too much about getting good grades in school. He was very mischievous and got into lots of trouble with his friends, but he always loved to read history and was fascinated by current events.

Upon graduating from Harvard, he enlisted in World War II as a PT-boat commander in the South Pacific. While on patrol on the night of August 2, 1943, the *PT-109* was rammed by a Japanese destroyer and exploded into flames, throwing crew members into the burning water. Two were killed and one was burned so badly he couldn't swim. Clutching a strap of the injured man's life jacket in his teeth, my father towed the wounded sailor to the nearest island, three miles away. For the next six days, with little food or water, the men hid, fearing they would be captured by the Japanese. Each evening he swam through the shark-infested waters to other islands seeking help. One day he was spotted by two Solomon Islanders. My father carved a message onto a coconut shell, which they took to the hideout of an Australian coast watcher who arranged rescue. When John F. Kennedy returned home, he was awarded the Navy and Marine Corps Medal for his leadership and courage.

With the war finally coming to an end, it was time to choose the kind of work he wanted to do. My father had first considered becoming a teacher or a writer, but because of his interest in government and history, he decided to run for Congress in Massachusetts' eleventh congressional district, where he won in 1946. He served for six years before being elected to a seat in the U.S. Senate.

While he was serving in the Senate, my father continued to study and think about what qualities are important in our leaders. Ever since he was a child, he had loved to read history and the biographies of his political heroes. He decided that moral courage was the quality he admired most. He wrote a book about eight of our greatest senators, men who had put the national interest ahead of their own careers. The book was called *Profiles in Courage*, and it won the Pulitzer Prize in 1957.

As the 1960 election approached, my father made the decision to run for president. Like many other young men of his generation, he had come home from the war believing in his ability to lead and eager to help build a dynamic postwar America. His campaign promised a New Frontier of challenges for America and energized a new generation of young Americans to get involved.

My father won the election by the closest margin ever: one-tenth of one percent. It was so close that, in terms of numbers (not the electoral college, which he won decisively), if one person in each precinct had voted the other way, his opponent would have won.

The night before the inauguration, there had been a giant blizzard in Washington, D.C. No one was sure that the ceremony would be able to take place on time. But the army spent most of the night removing the snow, and the morning was clear, cold, and sparkling. Thousands of people who came to watch felt as if the old world had been covered over and something new was about to begin. They were right.

John F. Kennedy succeeded Dwight D. Eisenhower, one of the oldest men ever to serve as president, a midwestern Republican and five-star general who had begun his military career in 1911, six years before my father was born. Before the ceremony, the incoming and outgoing presidents met for coffee at the White House. There was some awkward conversation and then the two men got in the car for the ride down Pennsylvania Avenue from the White House to the Capitol. They were a study in contrasts that heightened the sense that one generation was giving way to the next and that history was moving forward.

On Inauguration Day, my father decided that he didn't want America to be thought of as only a military power; he wanted to show the world that American civilization had come of age. He believed that America was the greatest country in the world, not just because of our system of democracy, but because of our art and literature, too. He asked the great poet Robert Frost to compose and read a poem for the occasion, in the tradition of ancient ceremonies of state. But when Frost stood up to read the special poem he had composed for the occasion, the glare from the snow was so bright that he couldn't see the words on the page. No one knew what was going to happen. They were afraid he might cry. But Frost proceeded to recite from memory his famous poem about the history of America, "The Gift Outright."

When John F. Kennedy stepped forward to take the oath of office and deliver his inaugural address, the whole world was watching. He knew that this speech was his chance to win over the people who hadn't voted for him and unite all Americans. The rest of the world was captivated by this young man, but also unsure of what his presidency might mean to them. The pressure was intense.

My father had worked hard on the speech. He had studied the great speeches of the past, from Pericles to Abraham Lincoln. He knew he wanted his inaugural address to be short, and he wanted it to be great. He wanted to inspire all Americans to serve their country and help him solve its problems, and he wanted to reassure other countries that America could be counted on to strengthen and defend freedom and democracy around the world.

His inaugural address is only 1,364 words long. It took thirteen minutes and fifty-nine seconds to deliver. Yet no one watching will ever forget it. It contained the immortal words, "Ask not what your country can do for you—ask what you can do for your country." It inspired a generation of Americans and set the stage for his entire Presidency. It has gone down in history as one of the greatest speeches ever given.

All my life, people have come up to me and said, "Your father changed my life. No one ever had ever asked anything of me before, but I got involved because he asked me to." People signed up to serve in the Peace Corps, they marched for civil rights and worked for social justice, they volunteered to help fight poverty, to teach in schools and start health clinics in underserved communities, to work in government. My father served as president for 1,000 days, yet he inspired a generation that transformed America, and that inspiration lives on.

Today, we face another pivotal moment in history. America's challenges are just as great, both at home and around the world. We need people to help bring peace to this world and end the threat of terrorism. We need people to help educate our children and fix our failing schools.

We need people to preserve and restore our natural environment. We need people to help the disadvantaged and find cures for diseases. And we need courageous political leaders who can work together to solve our problems and inspire new generations to believe, as John F. Kennedy did, that politics is a noble profession. Each of us has something to contribute to improve the lives of those around us, and each of us has a responsibility to give back to this country that has given us so much. Studying history, looking inside ourselves and at the world around us, will help us each decide what that gift might be.

## THE GIFT OUTRIGHT
# ROBERT FROST

The land was ours before we were the land's.
She was our land more than a hundred years
Before we were her people. She was ours
In Massachusetts, in Virginia,
But we were England's, still colonials,
Possessing what we still were unpossessed by,
Possessed by what we now no more possessed.
Something we were withholding made us weak
Until we found out that it was ourselves
We were withholding from our land of living,
And forthwith found salvation in surrender.
Such as we were we gave ourselves outright
(The deed of gift was many deeds of war)
To the land vaguely realizing westward,
But still unstoried, artless, unenhanced,
Such as she was, such as she would become.

# THE INAUGURAL ADDRESS

**VICE PRESIDENT JOHNSON,** Mr. Speaker, Mr. Chief Justice, President Eisenhower, Vice President Nixon, President Truman, reverend clergy, fellow citizens, we observe today not a victory of party, but a celebration of freedom—symbolizing an end, as well as a beginning—signifying renewal, as well as change. For I have sworn before you and Almighty God the same solemn oath our forebears prescribed nearly a century and three quarters ago.

The world is very different now. For man holds in his mortal hands the power to abolish all forms of human poverty and all forms of human life. And yet the same revolutionary beliefs for which our forebears fought are still at issue around the globe—the belief that the rights of man come not from the generosity of the state, but from the hand of God.

We dare not forget today that we are the heirs of that first revolution. Let the word go forth from this time and place, to friend and foe alike, that the torch has been passed to a new generation of Americans—born in this century, tempered by war, disciplined by a hard and bitter peace, proud of our ancient heritage—and unwilling to witness or permit the slow undoing of those human rights to which this Nation has always been committed, and to which we are committed today at home and around the world.

Let every nation know, whether it wishes us well or ill, that we shall pay any price, bear any burden, meet any hardship, support any friend, oppose any foe, in order to assure the survival and the success of liberty.

This much we pledge—and more.

To those old allies whose cultural and spiritual origins we share, we pledge the loyalty of faithful friends. United, there is little we cannot do in a host of cooperative ventures. Divided, there is little we can do—for we dare not meet a powerful challenge at odds and split asunder.

To those new States whom we welcome to the ranks of the free, we pledge our word that one form of colonial control shall not have passed away merely to be replaced by a far more iron tyranny. We shall not always expect to find them supporting our view. But we shall always hope to find them strongly supporting their own freedom—and to remember that, in the past, those who foolishly sought power by riding the back of the tiger ended up inside.

To those peoples in the huts and villages across the globe struggling to break the bonds of mass misery, we pledge our best efforts to help them help themselves, for whatever period is required—not because the Communists may be doing it, not because we seek their votes, but because it is right. If a free society cannot help the many who are poor, it cannot save the few who are rich.

To our sister republics south of our border, we offer a special pledge—to convert our good words into good deeds—in a new alliance for progress—to assist free men and free governments in casting off the chains of poverty. But this peaceful revolution of hope cannot become the prey of hostile powers. Let all our neighbors know that we shall join with them to oppose aggression or subversion anywhere in the Americas. And let every other power know that this Hemisphere intends to remain the master of its own house.

To that world assembly of sovereign states, the United Nations, our last best hope in an age where the instruments of war have far outpaced the instruments of peace, we renew our pledge of support—to prevent it from becoming merely a forum for invective—to strengthen its shield of the new and the weak—and to enlarge the area in which its writ may run.

Finally, to those nations who would make themselves our adversary, we offer not a pledge but a request: that both sides begin anew the quest for peace, before the dark powers of destruction unleashed by science engulf all humanity in planned or accidental self-destruction.

We dare not tempt them with weakness. For only when our arms are sufficient beyond doubt can we be certain beyond doubt that they will never be employed.

But neither can two great and powerful groups of nations take comfort from our present course—both sides overburdened by the cost of modern weapons, both rightly alarmed by the steady spread of the deadly atom, yet both racing to alter that uncertain balance of terror that stays the hand of mankind's final war.

So let us begin anew—remembering on both sides that civility is not a sign of weakness, and sincerity is always subject to proof. Let us never negotiate out of fear. But let us never fear to negotiate.

Let both sides explore what problems unite us instead of belaboring those problems which divide us.

Let both sides, for the first time, formulate serious and precise proposals for the inspection and control of arms—and bring the absolute power to destroy other nations under the absolute control of all nations.

Let both sides seek to invoke the wonders of science instead of its terrors. Together let us explore the stars, conquer the deserts, eradicate disease, tap the ocean depths, and encourage the arts and commerce.

Let both sides unite to heed in all corners of the earth the command of Isaiah—to "undo the heavy burdens . . . and to let the oppressed go free."

And if a beachhead of cooperation may push back the jungle of suspicion, let both sides join in creating a new endeavor, not a new balance of power, but a new world of law, where the strong are just and the weak secure and the peace preserved.

All this will not be finished in the first one hundred days. Nor will it be finished in the first one thousand days, nor in the life of this Administration, nor even perhaps in our lifetime on this planet. But let us begin.

In your hands, my fellow citizens, more than in mine, will rest the final success or failure of our course. Since this country was founded, each generation of Americans has been summoned to give testimony to its national loyalty. The graves of young Americans who answered the call to service surround the globe.

Now the trumpet summons us again—not as a call to bear arms, though arms we need; not as a call to battle, though embattled we are—but a call to bear the burden of a long twilight struggle, year in and year out, "rejoicing in hope, patient in tribulation"—a struggle against the common enemies of man: tyranny, poverty, disease, and war itself.

Can we forge against these enemies a grand and global alliance, North and South, East and West, that can assure a more fruitful life for all mankind? Will you join in that historic effort?

In the long history of the world, only a few generations have been granted the role of defending freedom in its hour of maximum danger. I do not shrink from this responsibility—I welcome it. I do not believe that any of us would exchange places with any other people or any other generation. The energy, the faith, the devotion which we bring to this endeavor will light our country and all who serve it—and the glow from that fire can truly light the world.

And so, my fellow Americans: ask not what your country can do for you—ask what you can do for your country.

My fellow citizens of the world: ask not what America will do for you, but what together we can do for the freedom of man.

Finally, whether you are citizens of America or citizens of the world, ask of us the same high standards of strength and sacrifice which we ask of you. With a good conscience our only sure reward, with history the final judge of our deeds, let us go forth to lead the land we love, asking His blessing and His help, but knowing that here on earth God's work must truly be our own.

# ELIZABETH PARTRIDGE

**JOHN F. KENNEDY** wanted to be President of the United States. He knew it was a long shot. He was only forty-two years old in 1959, when he considered running. People would say he was too young, and too inexperienced, to handle the challenges facing the nation. Besides, he was an Irish Catholic, and the United States had never elected a Catholic president. But he'd served in Congress for twelve years and seen enormous, exciting changes in America since World War II. Maybe the time was right for a candidate like him.

During the 1950s, Americans had become

more prosperous than ever before. Servicemen and -women had returned from the war eager to begin the next chapter of their lives. They had gone back to school on the GI Bill, or taken out loans for homes, farms, and businesses. They'd married and moved out of the cities and into the suburbs. American factories, never bombed during the war like the factories in Europe, led the world in producing steel, cars, and electrical appliances.

For the first time ever, most middle-class families owned homes, and had a refrigerator, a television, and a car. Some homes even had a brand-new Princess Phone in the master bedroom, to supplement the family telephone installed in the hallway.

Schools, libraries, and shopping malls were being built at a breakneck pace to handle all the children being born in the postwar "baby boom." Magazines were full of new ads for expensive watches and pens, perfume, cologne, and electric shavers. Women who'd worked during the war and were now home could see hundreds of ads for frosting and cake mixes, toasters, electric mixers, and coffee percolators—all portrayed by the magazines as essential items for smart homemakers.

People had leisure time and extra money, and wanted to be entertained. On their new black-and-white televisions, they watched shoot-'em-up Westerns like *Bonanza* and *Rawhide*, and sitcoms like *Leave It to Beaver* and *Father Knows Best*, with idealized, all-American families.

In the new shopping malls and on revived Main Streets, people bought records and went to the movies. Elvis Presley's single, "A Big Hunk o' Love," hit number one on the charts, and "Dream Lover" by Bobby Darin became a multimillion dollar seller. The epic film *Ben-Hur* smashed all records, winning eleven Academy Awards, and Marilyn Monroe's new comedy, *Some Like It Hot*, scooped up three Golden Globe Awards.

The cars rolling off the assembly lines in Detroit were big gas-guzzlers, but at twenty-five cents a gallon, it was cheap to fill up. Americans were encouraged to jump in their cars and "See the USA." In these heady days, anything seemed possible. Even our borders were expanding, as we welcomed Alaska and Hawaii as the forty-ninth and fiftieth states.

Kennedy bet that in this exhilarating time, voters would want members of his generation—those who'd come home from the war, established careers, and started families—to lead the country into the 1960s. On January 2, 1960, he announced he was running for president as a Democratic candidate. Richard Nixon, the Republican vice president, would run against him.

Kennedy crisscrossed the country in his campaign plane. He assured people that he would not only keep up their standard of living but also make sure the economy grew at 5 percent, twice the rate it had been expanding since 1953. Americans liked hearing that.

But not everyone was enjoying the full opportunities of postwar America.

In the impoverished state of West Virginia, thousands of coal miners had recently lost their jobs. Kennedy campaigned hard in West Virginia. It was critical he win over the conservative, largely Protestant voters who viewed him with suspicion because he was a Catholic.

Dressed in his immaculate suit, he visited the coal mines where miners worked long hours in dirty, dangerous conditions for low wages. He spoke to the unemployed miners and their wives. At every opportunity, he let listeners know he believed in separation of church and state.

His wife, Jacqueline Kennedy, joined him to campaign in West Virginia. Kennedy's staff had counseled against having her. She was poised, beautiful, and well-educated. The campaign staff was afraid the West Virginians would be intimidated by her. But the Kennedys won them over. Like people across the country, the voters in West Virginia were captivated by the handsome couple and their young daughter, Caroline.

As Kennedy traveled the state, he was shocked

by the unpaved roads, rough shacks, and flimsy outhouses. In some parts of West Virginia, many people needed relief food supplies to keep from starving. Every month, the federal government distributed food to needy families. A poor family with seven children would receive five bags of flour, four cans of powdered eggs, three five-pound bags of cornmeal, eight pounds of shortening, four pounds of rice, and powdered milk. This had to feed all nine people in the family for a whole month. It simply wasn't enough. Across West Virginia, Kennedy saw hungry, malnourished kids. Families needed help.

Kennedy promised "vigorous action by the federal government" if he were elected. People in West Virginia dared to hope he could help make their living and working conditions better. One man who listened to him speak said afterward that he felt a little prouder of being an American. It was a feeling Kennedy would ignite again and again.

The coal miners weren't the only ones excluded from the American dream. Another group Kennedy was determined to win over were African Americans, who often voted Republican. Kennedy needed to gain their confidence and their votes.

Just weeks after Kennedy had announced his campaign, four black students sat peacefully at a lunch counter in Greensboro, North Carolina, and asked to be served. They wanted to be allowed to eat at the counter with whites. In the segregated South, the sit-ins spread like wildfire to other "whites only" places: lunch counters, swimming pools, public parks, libraries, and beaches. African Americans were tired of waiting for change, tired of being second class citizens, tired of their children being in separate, inadequate schools, despite a 1954 Supreme Court ruling outlawing segregation in public schools.

In June, Kennedy invited Martin Luther King, Jr., for a meeting at his Manhattan apartment. Kennedy needed to reassure not only blacks but skeptical white liberals that he believed in civil rights. During the hour and a half meeting, Kennedy sought to reassure Dr. King that civil rights for African Americans was important to him.

A few months later, with the presidential campaign in full swing, Dr. King was arrested at a sit-in in Atlanta. Convicted of probation violation for an earlier charge of driving with an invalid license, he was sent, handcuffed and chained, to Georgia State Prison for a four-month sentence. The white authorities were determined to make an example of him.

Dr. King's family appealed to both Kennedy and Nixon for help with the unfair sentence. Nixon refused to comment. He didn't want to risk alienating any of the white Southern segregationists. But Kennedy immediately called Coretta Scott King to show his support. He had his brother, Robert Kennedy, follow up with phone calls to the judge and governor. In a few days, King was released.

Kennedy's campaign workers wanted to make sure African Americans across the South knew the part Kennedy had played in winning Dr. King's freedom. In the weeks before the election, they distributed thousands of flyers in the black community, contrasting "No Comment Nixon" to "A Candidate with a Heart, Senator Kennedy."

But a dark cloud hung over all Americans, white or black, rich or poor, and dominated the campaign. The United States and the Soviet Union had emerged from World War II as the two big "superpowers." The Communist government of the Soviet Union gave aid and military assistance to Communist revolutions worldwide. America was determined to block Communism from spreading to other countries.

As tensions grew between the Soviet Union and the United States, they locked into a permanent state of conflict, dubbed the Cold War. Neither side officially declared war on the other. Instead, they put out massive amounts of propaganda, spied on each other, and instituted trade restrictions and sanctions. The two superpowers poured money and military support into devastating "proxy wars" in Southeast Asia, Latin America, and many other places.

Scientists on both sides worked to develop larger, more powerful nuclear bombs that each country threatened to use against the other. In 1957, the Soviets had been the first to launch an intercontinental ballistic missile (ICBM). It could carry nuclear warheads more than 3,500 miles. Now American cities were within easy striking range of Soviet missiles.

A few months later the Soviets launched the world's first artificial satellite, *Sputnik*, into space. About the size of a basketball, it orbited the Earth every ninety-eight minutes, emitting a signal that could be tracked by radio.

*Sputnik* fascinated Americans. It was obvious the Soviets were far ahead in technology. From grammar schools to universities, millions of dollars were quickly allocated to teach math and science. Universities revved up their aerospace engineering programs. Telescopes and chemistry kits flew off the shelves of toy stores as families caught the excitement.

But *Sputnik* also terrified Americans. The

world felt more vulnerable than ever to attack, as the nuclear arms race and the space race between the two countries hit a furious pace. Dire predictions were everywhere. The world was on the edge of annihilation. Cities would be destroyed, and millions would die. Nuclear fallout would poison the world. More than half of all Americans believed that war with the Soviet Union was inevitable.

Civil defense sirens were mounted on top of buildings and programmed to give a prolonged, eight-minute howl of warning in case of nuclear attack. People were encouraged to build cement fallout shelters in their basements and backyards. The new schools held air raid drills, and children were taught to "duck and cover" under their desks until it was safe to come out. None of these would have been any help against a nuclear attack.

Americans wanted their leaders to be tough and stand up to the Soviet Union, but were terrified of the destruction that would result from an all-out war. Kennedy had to walk a fine line. He pledged he would never authorize the use of nuclear weapons in a first strike, but would only use them defensively. He believed negotiating a truce to the arms race was possible.

On September 26, 1960, Kennedy met with the Republican nominee, Richard Nixon, for the first-ever televised debate between two presidential candidates. Seventy million viewers tuned in. Kennedy spoke directly to the camera, and was relaxed, tanned, and well-informed. Nixon, recently hospitalized for an infection, was pasty looking, tired, and sweating under the studio lights. Television watchers felt Kennedy won the debate; those listening on the radio thought Nixon had won.

Throughout his campaign, Kennedy made a special effort to reach not only his generation, but young, new voters. He often spoke at colleges and universities, where students turned out in huge, gratifying numbers to see him. In October, he arrived incredibly late to speak at the University of Michigan. Ten thousand students were still waiting for him at two in the morning. He was exhausted and ready for bed, but in an impromptu speech, he challenged them to think not just of themselves. He asked them to serve their country and spend part of their lives working overseas.

In San Francisco just days before the election, he refined his thoughts further. He proposed "a peace corps of talented young men and women, willing and able to serve their country. . . ." It wasn't just rhetoric with Kennedy. He truly believed Americans, especially young Americans, had energy and talents they could share with others. The more they understood people in other countries, and the more others understood us, the more likely we were to have peace. It was by far the best weapon of defense, and a crucial step in negotiating peace.

Finally, it was November 8th, Election Day. All the hard campaigning was over. The race was too close to call. Kennedy gathered with his family and campaign staff at his father's house on Cape

Cod to wait for the election results. But even after midnight, it still wasn't clear who had won. Kennedy finally went to bed.

In the morning his daughter, Caroline, woke him up by saying, "Good morning, Mr. President."

Kennedy spent the next weeks preparing for the presidency: choosing advisers, reading books and papers, setting up committees, and working on his inauguration speech. He wanted it to be short, and inspiring.

It was. Despite his being elected by an incredibly narrow margin, the entire nation was electrified by his speech.

Kennedy got right to work as president. It was time to replace promises with action, and fear with hope. Less than twenty-four hours after his inaugural address, he signed his first Executive Order. It doubled the surplus food rations for West Virginians and other poor Americans, and included a wide variety of nutritious foods. A few weeks later, he signed an Executive Order establishing the Peace Corps, providing young

Americans a way to use their talents overseas.

During his administration, Kennedy would be challenged on every front. The Cuban Missile Crisis brought us to the very edge of nuclear war, and civil rights issues reached the boiling point in Birmingham, Alabama, when police turned police dogs and fire hoses on nonviolent protestors, including children. Kennedy negotiated America out of the Cuban Missile Crisis and introduced civil rights legislation into Congress. He set up a commission on the status of women and built up the Space Program. Despite setbacks, he was determined to move from confrontation to peaceful coexistence with the Soviets.

Kennedy had served just over one thousand days as president when he was assassinated on Friday, November 22, 1963. Not only the United States but also the world lost a great leader.

The outpouring of grief came from every corner of the globe. Many recalled the stirring words from his inauguration address as he set forth a call to action to the nation:

"All this will not be finished in the first one hundred days. Nor will it be finished in the first one thousand days, nor in the life of this Administration, nor even perhaps in our lifetime on this planet. But let us begin."

# REPORT TO THE AMERICAN PEOPLE ON CIVIL RIGHTS

## INTRODUCTION

When John F. Kennedy became president in 1961, black Americans, especially those living in southern and border states, were denied legal equality and human dignity. They could not vote, were barred from public facilities, were subjected to routine insults and violence (often carried out by law enforcement officials), and could not expect justice from the courts. Blacks were second class citizens, and the white South was determined to keep it that way. In the North, black Americans also faced discrimination (although it was more subtle) in housing, employment, and education. Civil rights leaders would ultimately confront the fact that racism was not simply a southern problem. But, from 1961 to 1963, the focus of civil rights activity was on the South. The fundamental prize sought by the civil rights movement of the early 1960s was something that black Americans had never known: full legal equality.

In the spring of 1963, Martin Luther King, Jr., organized desegregation protests in Birmingham, Alabama, which he called the most segregated city in America. The city administration, led by Police Chief "Bull" Connor, refused to yield. King mobilized sit-ins and marches by thousands of schoolchildren, beginning on Good Friday. Backed by the state's new segregationist governor, George Wallace, the Birmingham police used dogs and high-pressure fire hoses to put down the demonstrations. King was arrested along with nearly a thousand children. Kennedy, as a demonstration of federal authority, sent several thousand troops to an Alabama air base. The violence was broadcast on television to the nation and the world. The Kennedy administration moved rapidly to respond to the crisis by speeding up the drafting of a comprehensive civil rights bill.

The defiant Governor George Wallace, who had vowed at his inauguration to defend "segregation now, segregation tomorrow, and segregation forever," carried out his promise to "stand in the schoolhouse door" in June to prevent two black students from enrolling at the University of Alabama. On June 11, President Kennedy federalized the Alabama National Guard in order to protect the students and secure their admission. That evening, he addressed the nation about civil rights and defined the crisis as moral, announcing that major civil rights legislation would be submitted to the Congress to guarantee equal access to public facilities, to end segregation in education, and to provide federal protection of the right to vote.

## THE ADDRESS

Good evening my fellow citizens:

This afternoon, following a series of threats and defiant statements, the presence of Alabama National Guardsmen was required on the University of Alabama to carry out the final and unequivocal order of the United States District Court of the Northern District of Alabama. That order called for the admission of two clearly qualified young Alabama residents who happened to have been born Negro.

That they were admitted peacefully on the campus is due in good measure to the conduct of the students of the University of Alabama, who met their responsibilities in a constructive way.

I hope that every American, regardless of where he lives, will stop and examine his conscience about this and other related incidents. This Nation was founded by men of many nations and backgrounds. It was founded on the principle that all men are created equal, and that the rights of every man are diminished when the rights of one man are threatened.

Today we are committed to a worldwide struggle to promote and protect the rights of all who wish to be free. And when Americans are sent to Viet-Nam or West Berlin, we do not ask for whites only. It ought to be possible, therefore, for American students of any color to attend any public institution they select without having to be backed up by troops.

It ought to be possible for American consumers of any color to receive equal service in places of public accommodation, such as hotels and restaurants and theaters and retail stores, without being forced to resort to demonstrations in the street, and it ought to be possible for American citizens of any color to register to vote in a free election without interference or fear of reprisal.

It ought to be possible, in short, for every American to enjoy the privileges of being American without regard to his race or his color. In short, every American ought to have the right to be treated as he would wish to be treated, as one would wish his children to be treated. But this is not the case.

The Negro baby born in America today, regardless of the section of the Nation in which he is born, has about one-half as much chance of completing a high school as a white baby born in the same place on the same day, one-third as much chance of completing college, one-third as much chance of becoming a professional man, twice as much chance of becoming unemployed, about one-seventh as much chance of earning $10,000 a year, a life expectancy which is seven years shorter, and the prospects of earning only half as much.

This is not a sectional issue. Difficulties over segregation and discrimination exist in every city, in every State of the Union, producing in many cities a rising tide of discontent that threatens the public safety. Nor is this a partisan issue. In a time of domestic crisis men of good will and generosity should be able to unite regardless of party or politics. This is not even a legal or legislative issue alone. It is better to settle these matters in the courts than on the streets, and new laws are needed at every level, but law alone cannot make men see right.

We are confronted primarily with a moral issue. It is as old as the scriptures and is as clear as the American Constitution.

The heart of the question is whether all Americans are to be afforded equal rights and equal opportunities, whether we are going to treat our fellow Americans as we want to be treated. If an American, because his skin is dark, cannot eat lunch in a restaurant open to the public, if he cannot send his children to the best public school available, if he cannot vote for the public officials who will represent him, if, in short, he cannot enjoy the full and free life which all of us want, then who among us would be content to have the color of his skin changed and stand in his place? Who among us would then be content with the counsels of patience and delay?

One hundred years of delay have passed since

President Lincoln freed the slaves, yet their heirs, their grandsons, are not fully free. They are not yet freed from the bonds of injustice. They are not yet freed from social and economic oppression. And this Nation, for all its hopes and all its boasts, will not be fully free until all its citizens are free.

We preach freedom around the world, and we mean it, and we cherish our freedom here at home, but are we to say to the world, and much more importantly, to each other that this is the land of the free except for the Negroes; that we have no second-class citizens except Negroes; that we have no class or caste system, no ghettoes, no master race except with respect to Negroes?

Now the time has come for this Nation to fulfill its promise. The events in Birmingham and elsewhere have so increased the cries for equality that no city or State or legislative body can prudently choose to ignore them.

The fires of frustration and discord are burning in every city, North and South, where legal remedies are not at hand. Redress is sought in the streets, in demonstrations, parades, and protests which create tensions and threaten violence and threaten lives.

We face, therefore, a moral crisis as a country and as a people. It cannot be met by repressive police action. It cannot be left to increased demonstrations in the streets. It cannot be quieted by token moves or talk. It is time to act in the Congress, in your State and local legislative body and, above all, in all of our daily lives.

It is not enough to pin the blame on others, to say this is a problem of one section of the country or another, or deplore the fact that we face. A great change is at hand, and our task, our obligation, is to make that revolution, that change, peaceful and constructive for all.

Those who do nothing are inviting shame as well as violence. Those who act boldly are recognizing right as well as reality.

Next week I shall ask the Congress of the United States to act, to make a commitment it has not fully made in this century to the proposition that race has no place in American life or law. The Federal judiciary has upheld that proposition in the conduct of its affairs, including the employment of Federal personnel, the use of Federal facilities, and the sale of federally financed housing.

But there are other necessary measures which only the Congress can provide, and they must be provided at this session. The old code of equity law under which we live commands for every wrong a remedy, but in too many communities, in too many parts of the country, wrongs are inflicted on Negro citizens and there are no remedies at law. Unless the Congress acts, their only remedy is in the street.

I am, therefore, asking the Congress to enact legislation giving all Americans the right to be served in facilities which are open to the public—hotels, restaurants, theaters, retail stores, and similar establishments.

This seems to me to be an elementary right. Its denial is an arbitrary indignity that no

American in 1963 should have to endure, but many do. . . .

My fellow Americans, this is a problem which faces us all—in every city of the North as well as the South. Today there are Negroes unemployed, two or three times as many compared to whites, inadequate in education, moving into the large cities, unable to find work, young people particularly out of work without hope, denied equal rights, denied the opportunity to eat at a restaurant or lunch counter or go to a movie theater, denied the right to a decent education, denied almost today the right to attend a State university even though qualified. It seems to me that these are matters which concern us all, not merely Presidents or Congressmen or Governors, but every citizen of the United States.

This is one country. It has become one country because all of us and all the people who came here had an equal chance to develop their talents.

We cannot say to 10 percent of the population that you can't have that right; that your children cannot have the chance to develop whatever talents they have; that the only way that they are going to get their rights is to go into the streets and demonstrate. I think we owe them and we owe ourselves a better country than that.

Therefore, I am asking for your help in making it easier for us to move ahead and to provide the kind of equality of treatment which we would want ourselves; to give a chance for every child to be educated to the limit of his talents. . . .

This is what we are talking about and this is a matter which concerns this country and what it stands for, and in meeting it I ask the support of all our citizens.

Thank you very much.

# COMMENCEMENT ADDRESS AT AMERICAN UNIVERSITY

## INTRODUCTION

In the summer of 1962, Soviet premier Nikita Khrushchev reached a secret agreement with Fidel Castro to supply Cuba with nuclear missiles capable of reaching the United States, ostensibly for protecting the island against an American-sponsored invasion. In mid-October, American spy planes photographed the missile sites while still under construction. Kennedy and his advisers agreed to place a naval blockade around Cuba while demanding the removal of the missiles and the destruction of the sites. During these thirteen days in October 1962, the United States and the Soviet Union came the closest to nuclear war that the world has ever witnessed. Khrushchev, recognizing that the crisis could easily escalate into nuclear war, finally agreed to remove the missiles in return for an American pledge not to invade Cuba.

Following the peaceful resolution of the Cuban Missile Crisis in October 1962, President Kennedy and Premier Khrushchev sought to reduce tensions between their two nations. Both leaders realized they had come dangerously close to nuclear war. As Khrushchev described it, "The two most powerful nations had been squared off against each other, each with its finger on the button." JFK shared this concern, once remarking at a White House meeting, "It is insane that two men, sitting on opposite sides of the world, should be able to decide to bring an end to civilization."

In a series of private letters, Khrushchev and Kennedy reopened a dialogue on banning nuclear testing.

President Kennedy began to feel in the spring of 1963 that there was a possibility for some kind of new movement in our relations with the Soviet Union, and he began to look for an opportunity to make a "peace speech."

The following speech was delivered by President Kennedy on June 10, 1963, as the commencement address at American University. In this speech, he called on the Soviet Union to work with the United States to achieve a nuclear test ban treaty and help reduce the considerable international tensions and the specter of nuclear war at that time. He boldly called for an end to the Cold War. The Soviet government broadcast a translation of Kennedy's entire speech, and allowed it to be reprinted in the controlled Soviet press.

## THE ADDRESS

. . . I have chosen this time and this place to discuss . . . the most important topic on earth: world peace.

What kind of peace do I mean? What kind of peace do we seek? Not a Pax Americana enforced on the world by American weapons of war. Not the peace of the grave or the security of the slave. I am talking about genuine peace, the kind of peace that makes life on earth worth living, the kind that enables men and nations to grow and to hope and to build a better life for their children— not merely peace for Americans but peace for all men and women—not merely peace in our time but peace for all time.

I speak of peace because of the new face of war. Total war makes no sense in an age when great powers can maintain large and relatively invulnerable nuclear forces and refuse to surrender without resort to those forces. It makes no sense in an age when a single nuclear weapon contains almost ten times the explosive force delivered by all the allied air forces in the Second World War. It makes no sense in an age when the deadly poisons produced by a nuclear exchange would be carried by wind and water and soil and seed to the far corners of the globe and to generations yet unborn.

Today the expenditure of billions of dollars every year on weapons acquired for the purpose of making sure we never need to use them is essential to keeping the peace. But surely the acquisition of such idle stockpiles—which can only destroy and never create—is not the only, much less the most efficient, means of assuring peace.

I speak of peace, therefore, as the necessary rational end of rational men. I realize that the pursuit of peace is not as dramatic as the pursuit of war—and frequently the words of the pursuer fall on deaf ears. But we have no more urgent task. . . .

First: Let us examine our attitude toward peace itself. Too many of us think it is impossible. Too many think it unreal. But that is a dangerous, defeatist belief. It leads to the conclusion that war is inevitable—that mankind is doomed—that we are gripped by forces we cannot control.

We need not accept that view. Our problems are manmade—therefore, they can be solved by man. And man can be as big as he wants. No problem of human destiny is beyond human beings. Man's reason and spirit have often solved the seemingly unsolvable—and we believe they can do it again.

I am not referring to the absolute, infinite concept of peace and good will of which some fantasies and fanatics dream. I do not deny the value of hopes and dreams but we merely invite discouragement and incredulity by making that our only and immediate goal.

Let us focus instead on a more practical, more attainable peace—based not on a sudden revolution in human nature but on a gradual evolution in human institutions—on a series of concrete actions and effective agreements which are in the interest of all concerned. There is no single, simple key to this peace—no grand or magic formula to be adopted by one or two powers. Genuine peace must be the product of many nations, the sum of

many acts. It must be dynamic, not static, chang-
ing to meet the challenge of each new generation.
For peace is a process—a way of solving problems.

With such a peace, there will still be quarrels
and conflicting interests, as there are within families and nations. World peace, like community
peace, does not require that each man love his
neighbor—it requires only that they live together
in mutual tolerance, submitting their disputes to a
just and peaceful settlement. And history teaches
us that enmities between nations, as between in-
dividuals, do not last forever. . . .

So let us persevere. Peace need not be im-
practicable, and war need not be inevitable. By
defining our goal more clearly, by making it seem
more manageable and less remote, we can help
all peoples to see it, to draw hope from it, and to
move irresistibly toward it.

Second: Let us reexamine our attitude toward the Soviet Union. . . . No government or
social system is so evil that its people must be considered as lacking in virtue. As Americans, we find

communism profoundly repugnant as a negation of personal freedom and dignity. But we can still hail the Russian people for their many achievements— in science and space, in economic and industrial growth, in culture and in acts of courage.

Among the many traits the peoples of our two countries have in common, none is stronger than our mutual abhorrence of war. Almost unique among the major world powers, we have never been at war with each other. And no nation in the history of battle ever suffered more than the Soviet Union suffered in the course of the Second World War. At least 20 million lost their lives. Countless millions of homes and farms were burned or sacked. A third of the nation's territory, including nearly two thirds of its industrial base, was turned into a wasteland—a loss equivalent to the devastation of this country east of Chicago.

Today, should total war ever break out again—no matter how—our two countries would become the primary targets. It is an ironic but accurate fact that the two strongest powers are the two in the most danger of devastation. All we have built, all we have worked for, would be destroyed in the first twenty-four hours. And even in the cold war, which brings burdens and dangers to so many nations, including this Nation's closest allies—our two countries bear the heaviest burdens. For we are both devoting massive sums of money to weapons that could be better devoted to combating ignorance, poverty, and disease. We are both caught up in a vicious and dangerous cycle in which suspicion on one side breeds suspicion on the other, and new weapons beget counterweapons. . . .

So, let us not be blind to our differences—but let us also direct attention to our common interests and to the means by which those differences can be resolved. And if we cannot end now our differences, at least we can help make the world safe for diversity. For, in the final analysis, our most basic common link is that we all inhabit this small planet. We all breathe the same air. We all cherish our children's future. And we are all mortal. . . .

To make clear our good faith and solemn convictions on the matter, I now declare that the United States does not propose to conduct nuclear tests in the atmosphere so long as other states do not do so. We will not be the first to resume. Such a declaration is no substitute for a formal binding treaty, but I hope it will help us achieve one. Nor would such a treaty be a substitute for disarmament, but I hope it will help us achieve it.

Finally, my fellow Americans, let us examine our attitude toward peace and freedom here at home. The quality and spirit of our own society must justify and support our efforts abroad. We must show it in the dedication of our own lives—as many of you who are graduating today will have a unique opportunity to do, by serving without pay in the Peace Corps abroad or in the proposed National Service Corps here at home.

But wherever we are, we must all, in our daily lives, live up to the age-old faith that peace and freedom walk together. In too many of our cities today, the peace is not secure because the freedom is incomplete. . . .

The United States, as the world knows, will never start a war. We do not want a war. We do not now expect a war. This generation of Americans has already had enough—more than enough—of war and hate and oppression. We shall be prepared if others wish it. We shall be alert to try to stop it. But we shall also do our part to build a world of peace where the weak are safe and the strong are just. We are not helpless before that task or hopeless of its success. Confident and unafraid, we labor on—not toward a strategy of annihilation but toward a strategy of peace.